INTRODUCTION

To DIFFERING DEGREES, states have started relaxing the strictest terms of the economic shutdown that federal and state authorities imposed on us in the face of mounting panic over COVID-19. Now we face a new problem: how to get people working again. My recent Broadside, *Getting America Back to Work*, addresses the need for free market policies to reignite the economy. This Broadside, *It's Time to Let America Work Again*, addresses more specifically what we should do or, more importantly, undo to release the yoke of government dependence and reignite the vibrant jobs market our virus response crippled.

The first and most crucial step: stop discouraging work. As protests across the nation have demonstrated, Americans want to get back to work. Their frustration with policies that restrict their ability to control their futures is certainly understandable.

This collapse was neither an accident nor the result of negligence, greed, or malfeasance. It was intentional.

Under threat from a lethal virus, we decided to shut down a thriving economy. Whether that course of action was justified will be a matter for debate. But the fact is that mere months ago, more people were employed than at any time in our nation's history, the unemployment rate was at a fifty-year low, there were more job openings than people unemployed, blue-collar workers were harder to find than white-collar workers, and wages for all workers were increasing at rates not seen in a decade. America's working class was thriving and looking forward to an even more prosperous future.

Then, in a matter of weeks, it was gone.

This collapse was neither an accident nor

the result of negligence, greed, or malfeasance. It was intentional. Because COVID-19 is spread by human contact, our government made the conscious decision to limit interpersonal contact to the extent possible so as to prevent the disease from rapidly spreading and overwhelming our healthcare system – as it had in nations such as Italy and Spain.

From retail outlets to manufacturing plants, thriving businesses were viewed as hotbeds for the spread of this disease. So, contrary to the essence of what makes America a great and exceptional nation, our government enacted policies specifically designed to stop people from working and to relieve the financial stress that might otherwise have compelled them to return to work prematurely.

At the state level, governors across the country prevented people from working by shutting down their workplaces, requiring that people stay at home, and allowing only "essential" businesses to remain open.

At the federal level, to provide for people who were thereby unemployed, the government enacted legislation that: (i) created extremely generous unemployment insurance benefits pursuant to which many people made more money staying home than working; (ii) provided government checks to qualified taxpayers; and (iii) required small business owners (with under five hundred employees) to provide employees with paid sick leave or expanded family and medical leave for reasons related to COVID-19. The individuals covered included not only those who were ill but also those who needed to care for the ill or who needed to stay home and care for their children when schools were closed.

Since the goal was assisting people through the crisis and assuring that they did not feel the need to return to work prematurely, these policies initially made sense.

But, as with most government action in the economic sphere, there were adverse consequences. First, as work became impossible and often less economically beneficial than simply staying home, both unemployment insurance claims and the unemployment rate soared, hitting historic highs. That was no surprise. It was the plan.

Unfortunately, there were additional unintended economic consequences that manifested themselves in terms of poverty, human suffering, and death. Forcing Americans to stay home without the dignity of a job, the security of a paycheck, or the opportunity to succeed exponentially increased the threat of suicides as well as drug and alcohol addiction, creating an ongoing crisis of death and despair.

We always knew the shutdown was a tradeoff between economic damage and slowing the spread of the disease. In this respect, the shutdown initially appeared to make sense. Some argue in retrospect that we went too far in slowing the spread of the disease, creating unanticipated ancillary damage. There is reasonable support for that belief.

But, confronted with the possibility that hundreds of thousands – maybe millions – of Americans would die, it is difficult to second-guess the government's actions. I have no doubt that President Trump and governors across our nation did what they believed was in our best interests at the time. It was a very tough call made at a time when reliable information was scarce and guidance from medical experts was inconsistent and changing.

Nonetheless, as the economic and humanitarian costs of the shutdown have grown, potentially spiraling out of control, the public-health risks have diminished. We are better prepared for economic activity today than we were in March. The coronavirus fatality rate has decreased meaningfully since the pandemic began as scientists have learned more about how to avoid infection and doctors have improved treatment and medication options.

In addition, our lives have changed. We are more aware of the risks and how best to prevent exposure. Until there is a vaccine or an effective therapeutic, we are all aware of the need to wear masks, avoid crowds, keep our distance, wash our hands, and keep them off surfaces. The need for vulnerable people to self-isolate will also continue. Should there be a second wave of infection, we will be better prepared.

Therefore, the time has come for those who are not high-risk to work, socialize, and circulate. The economy needs to begin breathing again to avoid the suffering and potentially irreparable consequences of a continued shutdown. The work-discouraging programs the government put in place at the outset of the pandemic were intended to address a crisis, not to increase government dependence once that crisis abated.

Just as there were tradeoffs in closing down the economy, there will be tradeoffs as we open it. But, given the adverse health consequences of a continued shutdown, the tradeoff is life versus life – not life versus money, as shutdown proponents claim. The worst thing we could do is continue preventing or discouraging work.

Rather, we need policies that reward work and hiring across the economic spectrum.

More often than not, this will involve the government simply getting out of the way – undoing rather than doing. But there are limited actions the government can and should take. Targeted tax relief for individuals and businesses, and liability protection for businesses willing to open their doors, would certainly help get us on track to restoring economic vitality.

Ironically, the Democratic governors, senators, and representatives who advocate for continuing the current work-discouraging policies are also the ones who most vociferously complain about – and attempt to take political advantage of – the resulting high unemployment rate and decline in economic growth.

To their dismay and frustration, May's jobs numbers were a testament to what can happen if we safely and responsibly reopen our economy. Through the end of May, twenty-one states had meaningfully begun that process (and without adverse health consequences). While economists had forecast that in May the unemployment rate would hit 20 percent or higher and that the economy would shed 8 million jobs, the Bureau of Labor Statistics (BLS) reported that the unemployment rate actually *fell* from 14.7 percent to 13.3 percent as the economy *added* 2.5 million jobs (the biggest one-month jobs surge on record) and the number of people unemployed fell by 2.1 million.

According to the BLS, "[t]hese improvements in the labor market reflected a limited

---

The time has come for those who are not high-risk to work, socialize, and circulate.

---

resumption of economic activity that had been curtailed in March and April due to the coronavirus (COVID-19) pandemic and efforts to contain it." Notably, the improvements took place before twenty-nine states, including the large economies of states like New York and California, had meaningfully started the reopening process.

As the states that have reopened demonstrate, it's past time to put politics aside and reopen our economy safely and responsibly – while we still have an economy left to reopen. At both the state and the federal level, it's time to stop discouraging and start encouraging work.

THE SHUTDOWN'S UNINTENDED CONSEQUENCES

Testifying on May 12 before the Senate Health, Education, Labor & Pensions Committee, Dr. Anthony Fauci, a leading member of the Trump Administration's White House Coronavirus Task Force, warned of the potential for "really serious" consequences from renewed coronavirus outbreaks should states reopen prematurely. But opening the economy too late would have "really serious" consequences of its own.

Of course, Dr. Fauci is an immunologist focused on the pandemic. His motivation is to limit the number of deaths due to COVID-19. Ultimately, that is how the future will judge his success. As we face this pandemic, it is certainly important to heed the advice of medical experts. But these experts are neither businesspeople nor economists, and it would be a "really serious" mistake to ignore the economic costs of their recommendations in terms of poverty, human suffering, and death.

President Trump stated that we cannot let the COVID-19 "cure be worse than the problem itself." Members of the media howled in predictable agony at the remark, but the essential point is indisputable.

According to a Federal Reserve Bank survey published in May, nearly 40 percent of people in households making less than $40,000 a year lost their jobs in March. Fed Chairman Jerome Powell observed that "[t]his reversal of economic fortune has caused a level of pain that is hard to capture in words, as lives are upended amid great uncertainty about the future."

While it's difficult to measure, the pain and suffering Americans are enduring due to the economic shutdown is unquestionably severe. According to a Kaiser Family Foundation health tracking poll released May 27, 31 percent of Americans are falling behind in paying bills and having difficulties meeting household expenses such as food or health insurance coverage due to the pandemic. Additionally, 16 percent of all Americans said that, because of the shutdown's impact on their finances, "they or someone in their household have skipped meals or relied on charity or government food programs since February." That includes an even higher 30 percent of Black adults and 26 percent of Latinos in danger of hunger.

Those pressures are impacting Americans' mental health. Census Bureau data from the Household Pulse Survey shows that, in May, about 34 percent of respondents had symptoms of anxiety or depressive disorder. That's up from 11 percent in the period from January to June of 2019. The younger the respondents, the more they are experiencing these symptoms.

Perhaps not surprisingly, the Food and Drug Administration recently added Zoloft, one of the most widely prescribed antidepressants in the United States, to its list of drugs in short supply as demand has increased due to the mental-health strains caused by the pandemic.

Shutdown-related anxiety and depression are having severe consequences. A recent study entitled "Projected Deaths of Despair From COVID-19," by the Well Being Trust and the Robert Graham Center for Policy Studies in Family Medicine and Primary Care, predicted that a massive number of Americans could die due to the shutdown "if we do not do something immediately." Labeling deaths of despair from drugs, alcohol, and suicide an "epidemic within the pandemic," the researchers estimated total deaths ranging from 27,644 (assuming a quick recovery, with unemployment having the smallest impact) to 154,037 (assuming a slow recovery and unemployment having the greatest impact).

The "Deaths of Despair" study's number one suggestion for avoiding these deaths: "Get People Working."

I have some personal insight into what working-class Americans are enduring due to the shutdown. As a twenty-five-year-old in 1975, I was the sole support for my wife and two young children, finishing college, and expecting to enter law school in the fall. The economic and emotional pressures were intense, but I had a job that allowed me to feed my family, pay our bills, and look forward to a better future. A sudden government shutdown resulting in the loss of my job and rendering me unable to feed or house my young family, let alone complete my education, would have devastated me.

It's hard even to imagine sitting home for months with those I loved, able to work but prohibited from doing so, our only source of income a government check. I certainly would have welcomed that check, but government largesse is a poor substitute for the dignity of a job, the security of an earned paycheck, and the opportunity to succeed.

Had I lived in a state that remained shut down or opened only at the margins, knowing that the risks for a healthy twenty-five-year-old from the virus were very low (a death rate of roughly 0.03 percent for people in their twenties), I am certain I would have joined the protests with other Americans fighting for the right to retake their lives. Had the economic lockdown persisted, I have no doubt that the associated frustration, despair, and misery would have taken a severe physical and emotional toll.

As such, I have not been in the least surprised that protests have arisen spontaneously across the country, from California and Washington to Michigan, New York, Pennsylvania, Texas, and Virginia.

Thankfully, under pressure from the

> *We need policies that reward work and hiring across the economic spectrum.*

public amidst deteriorating economies, all fifty states are now in some stage of reopening, with positive results as the May jobs numbers unequivocally demonstrate. Despite what you may hear from the Left, Americans want to get back to work.

IT'S TIME TO REOPEN

The primary objection to reopening the economy is that it could lead to a resurgence of the disease. But it is increasingly clear that ending the lockdowns and reopening the economy while continuing to isolate the vulnerable presents nowhere near the dangers shutdown-proponents claimed.

Georgia was one of the first states to reopen when Governor Brian Kemp eased restrictions by executive order on April 20, 2020. He rescinded the state's shelter-in-place order on May 1.

The Governor was direct in explaining his decision, stating that he didn't "give a damn about politics right now." Rather, he was acting for those who "put their whole life into building a business," those who "are at home, going broke, worried about whether they can feed their children, make the mortgage payment." His concern was for the "effects on our economy and these individuals from a mental health perspective, from a physical health perspective, and literally for people being able to put food on their tables."

Shutdown-advocates went into panic mode. The following day, *New York* magazine's "Intelligencer" website ran an opinion article entitled "Georgia Risks Second Coronavirus Wave With Sudden Reopening of Businesses." It described the Governor's decision as "a huge gamble for Kemp or a blunt decision that jobs and profits matter more than lives."

It concluded that "Brian Kemp is playing with fire. But in fairness, he never promised Georgians anything but recklessness from the get-go."

The Atlanta Journal Constitution ran an article quoting Dr. Harry Heiman of Georgia State University's School of Public Health saying he was "skeptical that Georgia was ready for a 'worst-case scenario' if the disease re-emerges." It also quoted Dr. Marc Lipsitch of Harvard University as predicting that "it's 'almost for certain' Georgia would be hit again by another wave of the disease."

The Governor's political opponents were also quick to criticize. The *AJC* article quoted Kemp's 2018 gubernatorial opponent Stacey Abrams as calling his approach "dangerously incompetent." The chairwoman of the Democratic Party of Georgia, Nikema Williams, said that Kemp's actions will "make this crisis even worse and put more Georgians at risk."

On April 29, *The Atlantic* ran an article titled "Georgia's Experiment in Human Sacrifice," warning in its sub-heading online that "[t]he state is about to find out how many people need to lose their lives to shore up the economy." The article dramatically concluded that "[b]ecause of how infections tend to progress, it may be two or three weeks before hospitals see a new wave of people whose lungs look like they're studded with ground glass in X-rays."

It never happened.

Little more than a month after Kemp's executive order, at a press gaggle in Atlanta, Vice-President Pence was asked to respond to critics throughout the media and the Left who ripped Kemp when the reopening process began. He responded: "Let's be clear: Governor Brian Kemp has proven them wrong every day."

So, what did happen? The Institute for Health Metrics and Evaluation, an independent global health research center at the University of Washington, produces a COVID-19 model that *The Colorado Sun* has described as "[p]erhaps the most widely cited coronavirus model out there." *The Washington Post* has described it as "America's most influential coronavirus model." It was last updated (before the publication of this Broadside) on June 10 and shows that daily COVID-19 deaths in Georgia peaked on April 20 at 37. By June 8, over six weeks later, (the last date for actual rather than projected numbers) daily deaths had *declined* by 35 percent, to 24.

As for the spread of the disease, the IHME model estimates that, on April 20, Georgia was experiencing 4,227 COVID-19 infections per day. That estimate declines to 3,711 by June 8.

One can argue about the accuracy of the numbers or the modeling. But against predictions of bodies piling up like cordwood in the hallways of overstressed hospitals, Georgia's numbers are certainly not getting worse as the shutdown supporters argued so vociferously. An article in *The Resurgent* queried, "Where Does Brian Kemp Go For an Apology?" So far, to my knowledge, he hasn't received one.

Florida was another a state that reopened

its economy earlier than most. On April 29, Florida Governor Ron DeSantis announced a plan to lift the state's stay-at-home orders the following Monday. According to the IHME model, daily COVID-19 deaths were 43 on April 29. By June 8, they had declined 30 percent – to 30.

As for the spread of the disease, the IHME model estimates that, on April 9, Florida was experiencing 3,691 COVID-19 infections per day. That estimate declines to 2,905 by June 8.

In a May 29 article entitled "Tracking what's happening in states as they reopen," ABC News reported the results of an analysis it did on the first twenty-one states to ease social distancing restrictions. Its goal was to

---

Shutdown-related anxiety and depression are having severe consequences.

---

determine whether doing so impacted the spread of COVID-19. It reviewed data from Georgia and Florida as well as South Carolina, Montana, Mississippi, South Dakota, Arkansas, Colorado, Idaho, Iowa, North Dakota, Oklahoma, Tennessee, Texas, Utah, Wyoming, Kansas, Indiana, Missouri, Nebraska, and Ohio.

The conclusion: "there were no major increases in hospitalizations, deaths, or percentage of people testing positive in any of the 21 states."

Stop Discouraging Work

As more states lift the lockdown restrictions, it is becoming increasingly apparent that they can do so responsibly, safely, and without the adverse health consequences shutdown-advocates predicted. Of course, avoiding those consequences requires that people observe safety and social-distancing protocols. The levels of compliance will differ by state and over time. There may well be mini-spikes or baby waves in various locales. Events – such as the recent mass protests against police violence – may also impact the spread of the disease. As Dr. Fauci recently stated, "[y]ou still have to practice a degree of caution and carefully go through the process of trying to normalize."

Nonetheless, as stated in *The Wall Street Journal* on June 11, "headlines about a coronavirus resurgence in the U.S. are overblown so far, and the bigger threat is keeping the economy in a coma." An article on the same date in *The New York Times* titled "Where Reopening Is Working" stated in its sub-heading that "many parts of the U.S. have managed to reopen while still reducing new cases." According to the *Times* article, "[n]ationwide, weekly deaths have fallen for six weeks in a row."

Bottom line, if people are willing to follow the safety protocols, there is no justification for policies that comprehensively discourage work. In fact, given the adverse health consequences of despair, depression, alcoholism, and drug addiction, the worst thing we could do is continue such policies. Yet that is clearly what the Democrats want to do.

The Democrats have made no secret of their intention to take advantage of the pandemic to advance their agenda. Rather than acting in the best interests of American workers, Democrats are attempting to distance workers from their jobs and economic independence. Their intention is to discourage people returning to work and slow the economic recovery – at least until after the November election.

While the state economic shutdowns had the greatest negative impact on jobs, the most job-discouraging policy Congress passed was the CARES Act's $600-per-week increase in unemployment insurance benefits, which should expire in July. There is a difference between helping people who are unable to work and encouraging people not to work.

A May 2020 working paper, from the Becker Friedman Institute at the University of Chicago, found that 68 percent of workers who are eligible for unemployment insurance benefits can make more on unemployment than working. The median replacement rate is a stunning 134 percent, with 20 percent of eligible unemployed workers receiving benefits at least *twice as large* as their lost earnings. As the paper states, "the CARES Act actually provides income expansion rather than replacement for most unemployed workers."

In a June 4 letter to Senator Charles Grassley on the "Economic Effects of Additional Unemployment Benefits of $600 per Week," the nonpartisan Congressional Budget Office estimated that extending the $600-per-week increase in unemployment benefits for six months, as the Democrats are advocating, would result in roughly five out of every six recipients receiving "benefits that exceeded the weekly amounts they could expect to earn from work during those six months."

As a result, "[e]mployment would probably be lower in the second half of 2020 than it would be if the increase in unemployment benefits was not extended," and, "in calendar year 2021, employment would be lower than it would be without the extension." In other words, if you pay people more not to work (as the Democrats propose), fewer will work. It's hard to blame them; work almost becomes unaffordable.

Small wonder that employers are complaining that, even with 21 million Americans unemployed, they are having a hard time finding people willing to work. Because quick-service restaurants have drive-through windows, allowing customers to purchase food with minimal human contact, many chains are doing well and seeing yearly sales increases even during the shutdown. But they are having a difficult time staffing the restaurants.

One franchisee from Southern California told me that "[t]here are areas in Orange County where you can't find anyone to work." Another franchisee from the Southeast told me that their summer applicant pool "has been cut in half." That's a departure from the norm as they typically "see a significant increase in applicants" in the summer. This year they were expecting "the cream of the crop in applicants" given "all the restaurants and retails establishments closed due to COVID-19."

Unfortunately, when trying to hire workers, small businesses are currently competing against extremely generous government benefits, when they should be competing against each other.

Americans understand the negative implications of having government dependence pay more than work. According to a national survey commissioned by America First Policies and released in June, 76 percent of Americans (including 67 percent of liberals) believe those who have lost their jobs as a result of the COVID-19 shutdown should receive unemployment benefits equal to or less than their previous wages. Only 15 percent support benefits that exceed those wages.

Under current law, this $600 weekly benefit expires on July 31. That is the plan. These benefits were a temporary measure to get us through the crisis. Yet Nancy Pelosi wants to

> *It is increasingly clear that ending the lockdowns and reopening the economy while continuing to isolate the vulnerable presents nowhere near the dangers shutdown-proponents claimed.*

extend it. In the straining-to-find-an-acronym "Heroes Entering Roles Of Education Service (HEROES) Act," House Democrats are proposing a six-month extension of this $600-per-week work disincentive.

Senator Ron Wyden (D-OR) has gone a step further, proposing that Congress make the $600-per-week benefit permanent until the unemployment rate declines. He would then phase it out over time as the decline continued.

Think about that. Wyden wants to preserve a program that is materially increasing the unemployment rate by discouraging work, and to phase it out only as the unemployment rate it is causing to increase declines. Under his plan, that could well be never. In fact, for the "guaranteed income" crowd, never is the intent.

Actively Encourage Work

Rather than discouraging work, it's time to shift our focus back to getting people working and businesses hiring. We need policies that will increase opportunity rather than government dependence. In addition to letting work-discouraging policies expire, there are work-encouraging proposals that would assist in this effort.

For example, Art Laffer's and Steve Forbes's proposed payroll tax holiday would encourage both hiring and work. White House Economic Advisor Larry Kudlow's proposal to allow companies to deduct from taxable income 100 percent of all capital expenditures in the year such expenditures are made would encourage businesses to invest. Senate Majority Leader Mitch McConnell's proposal for coronavirus liability protection would allow businesses to reopen with certainty and confidence.

The best of these proposals is clearly the Laffer/Forbes proposal to suspend the payroll tax for the rest of the year. Currently, the Social Security and Medicare tax takes roughly 7.5 percent from workers' paychecks, and another 7.5 percent from an employer's profits, up to $137,700 of income. Those who are self-employed pay the full 15 percent tax on their income, in addition to income taxes.

With 21 million people unemployed, suspending the payroll tax through the end of the year would both increase the take-home pay of the 137 million American who are already employed – rewarding work – and help get those who are unemployed back to work by making it more economical for employers to hire them. Because lower-wage workers pay more in payroll taxes than they do in income taxes, they would benefit most.

To reduce the threat suspending social security taxes could have on the "trust funds" available to pay social security benefits, the Laffer/Forbes plan contemplates that the government transfer money from the general fund to cover any potential shortfall in the affected programs, as happened when both the Bush and Obama administrations similarly suspended payroll taxes.

Some complain that this tax cut fails to benefit the unemployed. While the intent is admittedly to reward work and encourage workers, this plan helps the unemployed in ways that increased unemployment benefits never could by creating jobs and increased wages. It would create jobs by simply reducing the costs of hiring workers. The more jobs the economy creates, the more businesses compete for employees. This, of course, materially drives up wages, as occurred for nineteen consecutive months before the pandemic hit our shores.

To quote President Obama, "[t]he best antipoverty program is a job." Suspending the payroll tax through the end of this year would create a whole lot of them. This proposal has the support of 70 percent of Americans, according to a national survey commissioned by America First Policies and released in June. An April survey by McLaughlin and Associates similarly found 67 percent approval.

The government's response to the pandemic to date has essentially been to reward people for not working. As a result, and to no one's surprise, fewer people are working. Many people are reluctant to return to work as the benefits of not working are greater. Despite the Democrats' efforts, we need to return to the time when working paid more than staying home.

It's time to restore the dignity of a job, the security of a paycheck, and the opportunity to create a better future for ourselves and our families. Americans are willing and anxious to return to work. It's time to help them get there.

Conclusion

We've learned a lot about ourselves since the pandemic hit our shores. We're vulnerable in ways we never fully understood, and there is much we take for granted that we should not. For the first time, many Americans have experienced the impact of government dependence on the human psyche. We've seen firsthand the frustration and despair that is often prevalent in socialist countries, where government reliance is mandatory and where survival depends more on government largesse than on individual achievement.

Perhaps we've come to more fully understand and respect what we had in this nation before the pandemic struck: a prosperous, free market economy where a person could succeed or fail based on their initiative, determination, or creativity. It's not surprising that there is a widespread desire to return to those days.

But a serious threat has arisen in this process. To fight the pandemic, our government has assumed more power than at almost any time in our history. Millions of Americans who were formerly independent have, of necessity, become dependent. But we allowed that assumption of power in order to address a crisis, not to transform America into a nation where we permanently surrender our liberty and independence.

While there is a strong desire to break free of that government reliance, those who believe in the collective over the individual are determined to keep the shackles of government dependence in place for as long as possible. Their intent is to increase our government dependence until it's too late to break free.

They certainly aren't shy about it. Echoing many members of his own party, the presumptive Democratic presidential nominee, former Vice-President Joe Biden, has referred to the pandemic as creating an "incredible opportunity ... to fundamentally transform the country."

The past three months have shown us

> *As more states lift the lockdown restrictions, it is becoming increasingly apparent that they can do so responsibly, safely, and without the adverse health consequences shutdown-advocates predicted.*

what that fundamentally transformed America would look like – a nation of dependence, misery, despair, and depression. In other words, a typical socialist nation.

We did what we thought was best to fight a horrendous disease and reduced its devastating impact. Our intent was always to address the problem before us, not to create an opportunity to expand the power of government elites or to relinquish our hard-won freedoms.

In fact, Biden would further expand government with the Green New Deal and the taxes required to implement it. Should the Green New Deal become law, the ensuing economic devastation would make the coronavirus shutdown look like prosperity.

The time has come to throw off the government shackles and get Americans working again. Fortunately, the Democrats' efforts to expand government's influence appear to be evaporating as Americans start returning to work and retaking control of their lives.

We sacrificed our prosperity to protect our very lives. While we must abide by reasonable precautions and continue to protect the vulnerable – pending an effective therapeutic or a vaccine – it's time to break the government's hold on our futures and return responsibility for our destiny where it belongs: in the hands of the people.

It's time for America to get back to work.

First American edition published in 2020 by Encounter Books, an activity of Encounter for Culture and Education, Inc., a nonprofit, tax exempt corporation. Encounter Books website address: www.encounterbooks.com

Manufactured in the United States and printed on acid-free paper. The paper used in this publication meets the minimum requirements of ANSI / NISO z39.48–1992 (R 1997) (*Permanence of Paper*).

FIRST AMERICAN EDITION

LIBRARY OF CONGRESS CATALOGING-IN-PUBLICATION DATA
IS AVAILABLE